© 2000   Sunbury and Shepperton Local History Society

ISBN   0 905178 66 1

Published by : Sunbury and Shepperton Local History Society

Printed by: Parchment (Oxford) Ltd.

Front Cover: (LH) Church Villa, Sunbury
              (RH) Shepperton House, Shepperton

SUNBURY AND SHEPPERTON LOCAL HISTORY SOCIETY

LOST HOUSES OF SUNBURY AND SHEPPERTON

A publication to mark the Year 2000

Jean Althorp and Pat Ward - Sunbury Text
Nick and Sue Pollard - Shepperton Text

ACKNOWLEDGEMENTS

The authors would like to thank the following for their help in this publication:

BP/Amoco (Sunbury) for sponsoring the publication
Hounslow Library
London Metropolitan Archive
National Monuments Record Centre, Swindon
Ordnance Survey
Public Record Office, Kew
Records Management Branch, Metropolitan Police
Spelthorne Borough Council, Planning Department
Surrey History Centre, Woking
Brenda & Keith Clifton
Mary Fitzhugh
Barbara Giles
Emily Harper
Carol Harris
Joy Hoole
Dr. Nicholas Pearce
Graham Smeed
Elizabeth Smeeth
Julia Thorogood
Maggie Tobin
Colin Squire (President), Nan Trimble (Sunbury Archivist) and Bert Brooking (Shepperton Archivist) of The Sunbury & Shepperton Local History Society

Photo Credits

p.13   Church Villa - Crown Copyright/NMRC
p.15   Duddington House - Maggie Tobin
p.23   Meadhurst House - BP/Amoco Ltd
p.45   Duppa's Farm - Joy Hoole
p.48   Fernleigh - Mary Fitzhugh
p.51   Halliford Bend (rh) - Crown Copyright/NMRC
p.52   Halliford Hoo - Crown Copyright/NMRC
p.54   Halliford House (top rh) - Mr & Mrs K.Clifton
p.58   Littleton Rectory - St Mary Magdalene Church, Littleton
p.60   Manor Farm - Crown Copyright/NMRC
p.65   White Cottage - Crown Copyright/NMRC

1185

All other photos - Sunbury & Shepperton Local History Society

Lost Houses of Sunbury & Shepperton
Contents

INTRODUCTION

The aim of this book is to mark the year 2000 by documenting some of the more notable houses which have disappeared from the Sunbury and Shepperton area, including under the general heading of Shepperton, the communities of Upper and Lower Halliford, Shepperton Green, Littleton and Charlton.

The choice of houses has been a subjective one, based on what were considered to be the most significant buildings, but also on the information available. Documentation on some of the houses which have disappeared over the years is very sketchy, and we would welcome comments from anyone who has further information.

Sunbury seems to have been particularly rich in large houses, many of which have made way for later developments; those in Shepperton were mainly Victorian and on a smaller scale. The reason for this is that Sunbury was popular in the 18th and 19th centuries as a pleasant riverside retreat for those who desired to build a large house close to London, but remain in the 'countryside'. Shepperton remained a much smaller settlement until the 20th Century, with only a few large houses near the river.

Most of the houses covered were demolished after the Second World War, and the 1960's seems to have been a particularly bad decade for the destruction of older houses. The reason is that increasing planning controls, and particularly the introduction of the Metropolitan Green Belt, meant that much less land was available for housing, and hence older houses built on large plots of land became attractive opportunities for developers. This process continues to this day, although buildings are now better protected through the listing system and the introduction of Conservation areas.

Rather than concentrate on the architectural aspects of the buildings, we have also tried to present the stories of the people who lived in them. We hope that this book will ensure that these houses, though lost, are not forgotten.

A NOTE ON THE SOURCES

Various sources were used during the preparation of this book, and are referred to in the text.

The primary source has been the archives of the Sunbury and Shepperton Local History Society, built up over nearly 50 years of the Society's existence and consisting of a great deal of information collected by members and others.

The census returns have been particularly useful in providing information about occupants of houses, but only between 1851 (the first useful census) and 1891 (the latest released to the public).

Directories, published throughout the 19th century and into the 20th, give lists of local 'gentry' and their residences in addition to useful local information such as shops, transport services etc.

The Valuation Survey conducted by the Inland Revenue between 1910-1915, to establish the rateable value of all property in the country, gives both information on occupiers and also (in most cases) detailed descriptions of the property.

Old issues of Ordnance Survey maps are invaluable for determining the position and layout of properties, and also give a clue to when they were built or demolished. Other useful maps include parish, estate, tithe and enclosure award maps.

Finally, we must thank those individuals and organisations who have lent photographs for copying - many photographs no doubt survive in private hands, their owners perhaps unaware that they hold the only record of a vanished building. The Society is always delighted to receive donations or loans of these precious reminders of our history.

Sunbury Houses

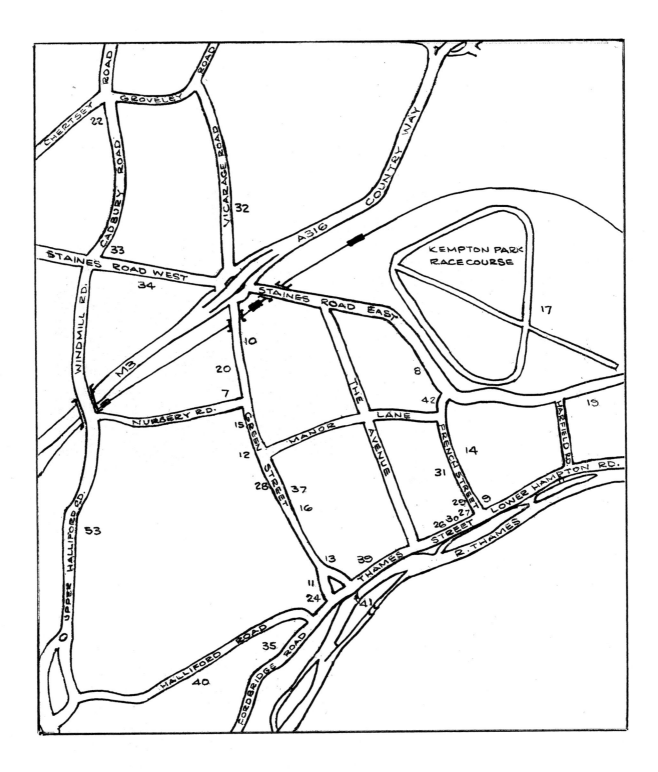

Numbers on the map refer to page numbers in the text.

The first mention of this solid Victorian house set in 3 acres was in 1865 when Joseph Boyce was in residence, and it was known as Aspen Villa. Various people lived there including Joseph Levin. The 1891 Census lists him as a printer and stationer, living there with his wife, Helen, and 2 sons, Harold a designer and Alexander a scholar. The longest occupancy was that of Leopold Weinthal who was there for at least 20 years from 1902. The house was sold by Harrods on 24th May 1927 with approximately two and a half acres of ground for £3000. A further one and a half acres was sold off for development. In 1933 the house was called Ravenscourt when Herbert Goodmans lived there. The house, which stood on the north side of Nursery Road, was demolished in the early 1960's to make way for the new houses built on the east side of Sunbury Manor School.

Batavia House

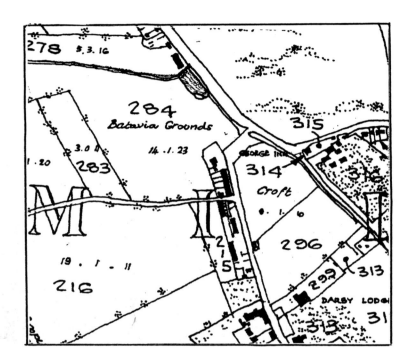

In 1711 Batavia House was described as the home of Sir Thomas Grantham who was said to have built a 'fair house' at Sunbury in 1697. The Sunbury Parish Vestry Minutes of 2nd June 1697 mentions that "Sir Thomas Grantham of ye parish of Sunbury in ye County of Middlesex Knt is now building a fair mansion house in ye Parish of Sunbury aforesaid to dwell in with his Lady and Family". It could have been a house similar to, but perhaps larger than, the William and Mary House in French Street. 'Batavia Grounds' was the name given to the land in the corner of French Street and Staines Road on the 1848 Sunbury Parish Map. The Grounds consisted of just over 14 acres given over to grass and was owned by Elizabeth Landon, but occupied by William Rolls.

Richard Penn in codicils to his Will in 1763 and 1768 mentions his house, Batavia House, in the Parish of Sunbury. He was the son of William Penn, the founder of Pennsylvania, and the father of Richard Penn, the deputy governor of Pennsylvania.

The house was demolished some time between 1768 and 1806. No reason is given for the demolition although this could have been connected with the fact that in 1806 the estate was split up and sold in lots. In October 1973, during excavations for the foundations for an office building to the east of Batavia Close, foundations of early 18th century brickwork were uncovered.

Beauclerc (formerly Rippledene) Lower Hampton Road

Rippledene was a large Victorian Italianate style house with its own boathouse, built about 1880. The photograph appears to show the garden front as there is a small flight of steps from the bay window to the lawn. The 2 wings appear to have been built at the same time as the main block, although the first floor of the wing to the right is much lower than that of the main building.

There was a local tradition that the house had been moved stone by stone from the south side of the river when the Metropolitan Water Board bought the land. This was confirmed in 1967 when the house was demolished, as the stones were found to be numbered.

This was a substantial house as the 1891 Census recorded James Matthews, a banker and prominent Freemason, his wife Sarah, 2 daughters, 4 sons, 2 visitors and 4 servants (cook, housemaid, nurse and page) living there.

In 1931 the house became a private school. The school had started in Bay Villas, Green Street about 1894, subsequently moved to a house at the end of the south side of Sutherland Avenue in 1906 and later still, moved to the Old Vicarage. On its move to Rippledene the name of the house was changed to Beauclerc. The house was demolished to make way for Beauclerc County Primary School.

Benwell House   Green Street

This was one of the last large Victorian houses built near the railway after the opening in 1864. It was a heavy Italianate building with windows from floor to ceiling and a brick portico to the front door, set in just over 19 acres of land, including the house, a cottage, gardens and meadow land.

The first recorded occupant was Arthur M. Mitchison in 1884 who lived in the house until at least 1890. He must have been related to William Arthur Mitchison JP who lived in the Manor House from 1852 to 1890. William Mitchison was a large landowner according to the 1848 Parish Map, owning all the land between Green Street and The Avenue, and from Staines Road East to Manor Lane, and a little way beyond. This included the land where the Manor House and later Benwell House were built.

Various other people occupied the house including Comdr. Hamilton Pym Freer-Smith RN in 1906. By 1914 he had become Sir Hamilton Pym Freer-Smith and lived there for at least 20 years. Miss Chataway who lived at Manor Cottage had fond memories of attending Balls at the house during this period.

In 1932 Sunbury Urban District Council, who had outgrown their premises in Church Villa, bought the house for Council Offices, but in 1984 it was demolished when Spelthorne Council moved all the offices to Knowle Green, Staines. The portico was rescued and is now the north gate to the Walled Garden, Sunbury Park.

This 18th century house was built sideways flush onto the road with an entrance straight into the hall. The 1848 Parish Map shows it was owned by the heirs of John Bishop and occupied by Tabitha Hubbard. Various people lived there including James Tucker who is listed on the 1881 Census. He was there with his wife Frances, 5 daughters and 4 servants.

By 1891 Sidney George Higgins, Company Secretary, had moved in with his wife Ida (both of whom were 24) his mother-in-law, sister-in-law and 2 servants (page and cook). The 1912 Valuation Survey says that Sidney Higgins was the occupier and his wife Ida was the owner. By 1922 Sidney had become Sir Sidney Higgins CBE and in 1926 moved next door into Montford House. When Sir Sidney left, his brother Charles Jepson Higgins moved in and lived there for some years. Both Sidney and Charles are buried in Sunbury and have memorials in St Mary's Church.

In 1950, A. Cemus Davis owned the house, the freehold property having been sold to him for £6000. It was described as being a fine old period house with a lovely walled garden of half an acre. It had an entrance hall, dining room, drawing room, pantry, kitchen, scullery, store rooms, maids' sitting room, all on the ground floor. On the first floor were 3 bedrooms, 2 dressings rooms and a bathroom. Above, there were 2 more bedrooms and attic rooms. Outside was a stabling block used as a garage, with rooms above. The garden was well stocked with lawns, beds, pergolas and kitchen gardens.

Various planning applications were lodged with the Council between 1962 and 1963. The last one, granting 31 dwellings, meant Brooklands was demolished and the row of town houses, Brooklands Terrace, was erected. The old wall dividing Montford House and Brooklands still stands - it separates the Police College from the Terrace.

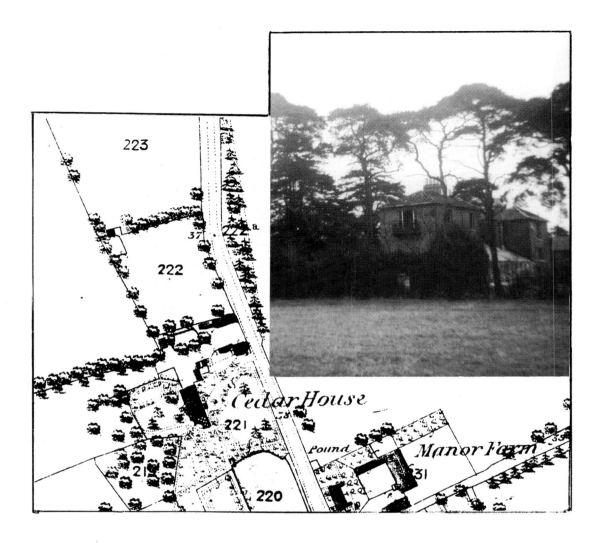

The Cedars Recreation Ground was once the extensive grounds of The Cedars. The house with 2 grass paddocks, together totalling about 9 acres, appear on the 1848 Parish Map and belonged to Henrietta Crump, but was occupied by John Smith Soden. In the 1861 Census, Captain George Gifford RN was in residence with his wife, Magdaline, and 6 year old niece, Myra Bayley, attended by 5 servants (lady's maid, cook, parlour maid, housemaid and groom). George Gifford was the son of Admiral John Gifford and had a distinguished career in the Navy. He served on a variety of 16 to 28 gun ships, was a Snr Lt in the Mediterranean and East Indies, saw action in 1841 in China and was later appointed to a steam frigate off West Africa in 1846. By 1856 he had become an Admiral and continued to reside at The Cedars until at least 1868.

Other residents included Col Fielder, Thomas Mitchell, a surveyor, Mrs Bond, and by the 1891 Census Alfred Harvey Willoughby, a young medical practitioner, his wife Lottie and 2 servants (housemaid and groom). Dr Willoughby was there until 1898, after which time Edward Wood moved in.

The last of the cedar trees, after which the house was named, was blown down in the Great Storm of 1987, but a sapling cedar has been planted in its place.

This was an early 18th century house first mentioned in 1839 when John Collingridge occupied it.

The 1861 Census shows William Church Bolt, son of William Bolt of Hawke Villa, living in Church Villa with his wife Mary, 4 young daughters and 2 sons. He ran a Boarding School here for 5 boys aged 8 - 11 years with the help of a tutor schoolmaster. As all his own children were aged up to 11 years they could have been educated alongside the boarders. The decline in numbers in the school in Hawke Villa could be connected with the opening of this new school. By 1871 the school had closed and on the Census day Louisa Bolt (widow of William Bolt) was in residence with 4 grandchildren, a visitor and 2 servants. Another 10 years passed and Mary Bolt (widow of William Church Bolt) lived there with 2 daughters and 2 sons, one a banker, the other a coal merchant.

By 1891 the house had become a Club as the Census of that year shows Joseph and Amelia Brooker residing there as steward and stewardess with their nephew and great nephew.

The newly formed UDC were looking for premises and took out a 21 year lease in August 1895 costing £45 a year, to use the house as Council Offices, and in 1896 the Sunbury fire engine and appliances were moved into the stables, again with a 21 year lease for £10 a year. The 1912 Valuation Survey records the owner as William W Bolton, secretary, Sunbury Hall Co Ltd, Willow Bank, Sunbury on Thames.

The original iron railings were still in place when it was demolished in 1968 to make way for the retirement flats. The Council Offices had been moved to Benwell House some years before, after which the church held a youth club there. Later the Fire Brigade moved into new premises in Staines Road West in 1965.

Darby Lodge   French Street

Darby Lodge was built on just over 1 acre of land carved out of the Darby House estate on the east side of French Street between Darby Gardens and Oakington Drive . It appears on the 1848 Parish Map and, although unoccupied, was owned by Maria Hayes.

The 1851 Census states that 3 unmarried sisters, Emily Hulme (39), Maria (38), and Matilda (34), all listed as fundholders, were living in the house with 3 servants. By 1861 Thomas Pavier, a landowner, was in residence with his wife Sarah. On the Census day their daughter Sarah and her husband were living in the house together with their new baby of 3 weeks, who was as yet unnamed. The household included a monthly nurse for the new baby and the 3 servants (cook, housemaid and groom).

By 1867 John Philip Fletcher had moved into Darby Lodge and lived there until 1903. He was 52 years old when he came and was the unmarried son of a Baronet BA, with his income derived from lands and dividends. An 1862 map shows a square house with a large bay in front and a large wing to the side and rear on the south east. There was an ice house in the grounds. Another occupant, Edward Bennett, also stayed a long time - from 1906 until at least 1926.

The 1912 Valuation Survey describes it as being a brick and stone residence, well fitted and decorated, with vestibule, hall, drawing room, dining room, study, billiard room, scullery, larder, pantry, cellar and school room, with 6 bedrooms above. The house was lit by electricity. In the grounds were stabling, loose box and 2 stalls, loft over double coach house and harness room. There were 3 glasshouses, a walled kitchen garden, paddock and walled front boundary. Most occupants seemed to have only 3 servants in this large house. It was demolished in the 1930's.

Duddington House   Green Street

Duddington House was first mentioned in 1878 when John Morris was in residence. The 1881 Census tells us that he was a builder and lived there with his 2 daughters, Elizabeth and Mary, his sons, Richard who was a clerk and Arthur, a clerk to a surveyor, together with one servant. By 1891 his 2 daughters were still living with him and another son Edgar, a solicitor was also there. By 1892 Edgar had taken over the property and continued to live there until at least 1902. In 1908 Col. George Grant was the resident.

The 1912 Valuation Survey gives a detailed description of the property and states that Col. George Grant was the occupier although it was owned by John Morris, Grosvenor Square, London. The house is described as a brick and stone residence with hall, dining room, drawing room, library, kitchen, scullery, pantry, WC and conservatory on the ground floor. The first floor had 5 bedrooms, bathroom and WC. On the second floor were 2 attics and a billiard room.

In the grounds were stables with 2 stalls and a loose box, a coachhouse with rooms over, cow shed and piggeries, all brick or stone built. The whole property covered just over an acre.

Various tenants lived in the house including Hugh Young Gibson who was there from 1926 to 1937. In 1947 a local builder, Mr. George Gamblin bought part of the land to the north of the house to build Heathlands Close. The coachhouse was on his land and he converted it into a house for his niece, Mrs Tobin. When looking for a source of damp a few years later the original cobble stones were found under the floorboards. A local resident remembers a lady living in the house on her own in 1948.

In 1949 the Health Service applied to the Council for permission to use the house as the local clinic. In 1971 the new Health Centre in Green Street was completed and Duddington House was then demolished. The house stood to the north of the main clinic where the car park and single storey building are now. (Map reference 224c.)

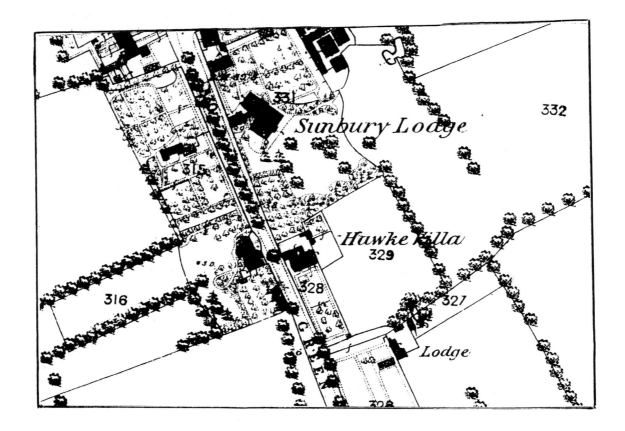

This early Victorian house was owned and occupied in 1848 by William Bolt. In the 1851 Census he was widowed and using the house as a Boarding School as he is listed as 'School Proprietor'. Living in the house were his daughter Mary, son James, who at 17 was a land surveyor, his 2 nieces of 19 and 18 and an assistant schoolmaster. There were 7 pupils, but only 1 servant, so it can be assumed that the daughter and nieces assisted in running the house. By 1861 William was 66 years old and had remarried. Mary was still at home but there was a different school assistant and only 3 pupils, together with 2 servants. (See connection with Church Villa.)

Various people resided in the house for short periods until the 1871 Census shows Charles Marshall, an architect, living there with his wife, little daughter and 3 servants. He stayed for a few years and by 1878 Edward Gordon, a member of the Stock Exchange, had taken over. He, in his turn, had by 1881 passed it over to another member of the Stock Exchange, James Ross and his wife Amy. It appears to have become a desirable residence for young professional people from London.

In July 1890 it was sold to Frederick Anthony Wallroth for £1000. It was demolished some time before 1915 as it appears on large scale OS maps until the 1915 edition.

Kempton Park

In 1851 a Gothic Revival house, said to rival the splendour of Strawberry Hill, existed on the site at Kempton Park. The estate covered 440 acres and was owned by Edward Raphael of Thames Ditton. The Census of that date shows that Thomas Taylor farmed the estate together with his wife Jane, 2 sons Thomas and John, and daughter Jane. It is interesting to note that there were 26 farm servants (male and female) only one of whom was English - the rest were Irish immigrants.

In 1863 Thomas Bennett and Peregrine Birch of Sunbury Lodge became partners in a property development and were later joined by Thomas' brother Edward of Kenton Court. In 1864 the partnership bought Kempton Park for £40,000 and intended to develop the area by building large detached and semi-detached villas, a few of which (now gone) were built on the Hampton side. Thomas Bennett must have rented the property first as the 1861 Census has him living there with his wife Sarah, 3 young daughters and 2 sons, he is stated to be a landed proprietor. Thomas built the Victorian house pictured here and a few years later the Gothic Revival house was blown up by the cadets from the Military Academy in Sunbury House (not very successfully as most of it had to be pulled down later).

Nothing came of the development plans and in 1872 the partnership members decided to sell up. In 1874 Peregrine Birch sold Sunbury Lodge and moved away; later in 1877 he sold out of the partnership. Thomas put Kempton Park estate on the market, sold it to Samuel Hyde and moved to Sussex.

Samuel Hyde, Secretary to the Bristol Racecourse Company bought the house and estate to develop a racecourse. In the 1881 Census, Samuel, described as an accountant, was living there with his wife Mary, 2 daughters, and 3 sons, one of whom was a clerk in an advertising office. Samuel was one of the original members of Sunbury Urban District Council and the first Chairman. When Samuel died in 1898, his son Walter took over and members of the Hyde family lived there until the property was bought by a business man before being sold to the Betting Levy Board. The house was demolished during later racecourse development.

* Possibly Thomas Barnett (see p.19)

17

Kempton Park

Kenton Court

Kenton Court (formerly The White House)
Staines Road East

Kenton Court was built of Suffolk brick about 1859 for Edward Barnett, of Burntwood Grange, Wandsworth. He was the brother of Thomas Barnett, of Kempton Park and later became a partner in the Barnett and Birch property development venture of which his house was the first to be built.

The 1881 Census lists Edward Barnett as a gun manufacturer living in the house with his wife Jaquetta, a son and 4 daughters. By 1891 the eldest daughter had left, but the son Edward was also listed as a gun manufacturer. There were 6 servants in the house (cook, housemaids, ladies maid, kitchen maid and butler). Although a partner in the property development, Edward still appears to be carrying on his family business.

By 1900 the Barnett family had moved and it was the home of Guy Boothby, the Australian novelist, author of numerous adventure stories, including 'Dr Nikola', which were very popular.

The 1912 Valuation Survey showed that Kenton Court was occupied by Willson Crosse, but was owned by Ada Barnett of Tunbridge Wells, the daughter of Edward Barnett Snr. The estate covered just over 26 acres and stretched from Staines Road East down to the river where Sunbury Sports Club is now. There is a very detailed description of the house which was well built with stone heads, mullions and cills, balustrading and a slate roof with lead hips and ridges. The first floor accommodation consisted of 9 bedrooms but only 1 bathroom, servants room, linen room, WC, 2 dressing rooms and a nursery room. The ground floor had an entrance hall, dining room, library, billiard room, morning room, WC and offices. There was a conservatory at the side, and brick stabling including 7 stalls, a loose box, harness room and coachhouse, 6 L-shaped heated greenhouses and 6 straight greenhouses. In addition there was a gardeners cottage and 20 acres of meadow land.

Towards the end of its life it was occupied by members of the original Barnett family - Major Barnett, who could have been the son who joined the family firm as he was now nearly 100 years old, and his 2 sisters. Before it was demolished in 1950, Emily Harper (a Sunbury resident) went there to visit the old housekeeper who was left in charge. She said the house was in a poor way and falling to pieces with chickens running around in the ground floor rooms.

Marion Park (formerly Mount Pleasant) Off Nursery Road

The house was built for Anthony Ponti Romano in about 1750 as a three storey Georgian building with a central doorway. Later an early Victorian two storey wing was added to the east. It is listed on the 1848 Parish Map as being occupied by John William Underwood and owned by John Allister. John Underwood used the house as a boys' academy and lived there with his wife, 3 teachers (maths, French and general teacher), 18 pupils (aged between 8 and 15 years), and 5 servants. In 1861 he was still there with 2 different teachers, only 8 pupils (aged between 12 and 17 years) and 5 servants (housekeeper, cook and housemaids). By 1870 it was called a collegiate school and run by the Rev. James Ledger Bere with his wife, son and daughter, 27 pupils and 6 servants.

Marion Park (formerly Mount Pleasant)   Off Nursery Road

By 1876 the school had closed and was sold in London on 19th July by Statham Hobson and Marner. At least 3 different people lived there until the house was purchased with 13 acres for £4000 for use as an orphanage in 1891.

The house became the Good Templars & Temperance Society Orphanage for orphans of total abstainers and was opened with a Matron, Hephzibath Cunningham, a governess, Adelaide Mathingley, 25 girls aged between 4 and 16 years, 30 boys aged between 5 and 13 years, and 4 servants (needlewoman, cook, laundrymaid and housemaid). It continued as an orphanage for about 60 boys and girls, by now under a Master and Matron, the first being Mr. and Mrs. V. A. Chappell in 1895, who stayed there until 1922. Between 1900 and the 1930's wealthy local people arranged parties and outings for the orphans, and photographs were taken of the Master and Matron with the children at annual garden parties.

At first the children had been taught in rooms in the house, but in 1908 the school was built in the grounds. After World War I the gymnasium was built as a War Memorial to old boys lost in the war. The orphanage continued to be run by a Master and Matron until World War II when the children were evacuated. After the war, as the building was found to be in a bad state of repair the children were moved to a temporary home in Purley and in 1949 went to a new home in Hampshire.

The house and land were purchased by Sunbury UDC and the house demolished in 1952 for the building of Sunbury Grammar School and later Sunbury 6th Form College. The only buildings retained were the School and the gymnasium which were used as overflow accommodation for Kenyngton Manor Secondary School and Springfield Primary School. Both buildings are still used by Sunbury Manor School.

GOOD TEMPLAR AND TEMPERANCE ORPHANAGE, SUNBURY ON-THAMES.

Meadhurst House   Cadbury Road

Meadhurst was one of the first houses to be erected on Sunbury Common after the inclosure of 1803, but before 1809 when it was marked on a plan as belonging to Mr. Allen. In 1917 the house, which had once belonged to the Cadbury family, was in a poor way, as it had been left empty after being occupied by Belgian refugees who were supported by voluntary contributions from the neighbours. The house had been sold by R. D. Morgan to A. R. Canham on 3rd November 1916. He in his turn sold it to the Anglo-Persian Oil Company in November 1917 for the creation of a laboratory run by Dr. A.E.Dunstan and Dr. F.B.Thole as research chemists.

In his memoirs Dr. Dunstan describes the house and its acquisition:-

"After much searching I discovered an old Georgian mansion, Meadhurst, containing fourteen rooms and a remarkably big semi-basement at Sunbury on Thames, with three acres of unrestricted freehold land attached. The price of this estate, really out in the country although only a mile from Sunbury station, was £937 in all. After all the legal formalities were completed, my wife and daughter, and Dr. Thole and myself constituting the entire research staff of the great Anglo-Persian Oil Company Limited, moved in and spent an exciting time turning the basement into a laboratory - reasonably up to date in its fittings and furniture and equipment with all the known appliances for the analysis of petroleum and its products."

The original laboratory in the basement had half a dozen people working there by 1919. As Drs. Dunstan and Thole lived in the house they often worked there through Saturdays and Sundays. By the end of that year it was realised that the working conditions were not suitable, so more land was purchased and a brand new research department built. Dr. Dunstan left Sunbury in 1924 to go to Head Office in London and in 1936 Meadhurst House was demolished, having outgrown its original purpose, and new buildings were erected. The name Meadhurst was transferred to the BP Sports and Social Club.

Photographs	Meadhurst House
(overleaf)	Laboratory with Drs. Dunstan and Thole
	Laboratory staff

Meadhurst House   Cadbury Road

Montford House   Green Street

This late 17th century house was owned and occupied by Joseph Fry who sold it in 1783 to Lord Montford, when it was then called The Manor House. On 31st January 1832 a lease was signed between William Maxwell and William Cobbett on land on this site for 700 years from 24th June 1831 for an annual rent of 1d (old money). The 1848 Parish Map shows that it was owned and occupied by Willian Cobbett and the property was described as house, garden, yard etc. on just over 2 acres. The Cobbett family continued to live here until the 1880's when William Horatio Harfield resided in the house for a few years.

Rivermead

Rivermead House was originally named Sunbury Villa when built in 1821 for John Collingridge. It was a typical stuccoed, bay fronted house of the Regency period with a glass conservatory at the front, the roof of which was supported by caryatids - it was then known locally as The Image House. The property consisted of the house, stables and eyot land. The garden extended west and included the gazebo which still stands in the corner of Dax Court gardens. In later years the conservatory was removed as is shown in the photograph.

In the 1861 Census the family of William Holland Furlonge were living in the house. On the Census day the parents were away from home and the 4 young children aged from 2 to 6 years were there being looked after by a Governess and a visitor to the family. There were 7 servants (dairy maid, laundry maid, housemaid, cook, nurse, coachman and gardener).

In 1865 the Bruce-Knight family had moved in, although by 1871 Richard Lamb, JP and landowner, was in residence with his 3 children and 10 servants. In 1876 Lord Brabazon the eldest son of the Earl of Meath took the house for the summer.

The 1912 Valuation Survey shows the owners as being Robert Knight-Bruce of London, Walter Moore of London and Mrs Caroline M. E. Knight-Bruce of Richmond, all trustees of the will of L.B. Knight-Bruce. The name 'Knight-Bruce' appears to be confusing to recorders as it is often transposed to 'Bruce-Knight'.

From 1926 owners applied for planning permission to convert or demolish the house. In 1926 an application was put in for converting to industrial use. 1950 it was used as offices, and in 1956 application was made for a restaurant and flats. In the 1960s it was owned by Major Morris who continued planning applications - 1962 for flats, 1964 for ten houses and lastly 1972 for flats which was granted and the house was demolished.

The Rookery   Green Street

The Rookery, built in the latter half of the 18th Century, was a typical large Georgian house with a hipped roof. Inside was a graceful staircase with delicate banisters. Records of mortgage agreements show that the grounds were extensive - 11 acres and 1 pole - with a frontage of 531 feet on to Green Street. It was insured at the end of the 19th Century with the Alliance Fire Insurance Company for £1200. The document showed that a claim would only be paid out if the policy and receipts for every premium paid were produced.

The 1871 Census shows Richard Dax, a barrister, living there with his wife Rose, a son, a daughter, 4 nieces and 3 servants. Later in the 1870s it changed hands until 1878 when Walter Scroton with his wife and 4 servants took over until at least 1882. The 1891 Census tells us that Frederick Marks, a young man of 28 living on his own means, was resident with his wife Eliza, 2 little daughters of 4 and 3, and 3 servants (nurse, cook and housemaid).

By 1897, The Rookery was occupied by Edward Butterfield who resided there until at least 1912. The 1912 Valuation Survey shows that it stood in just over an acre of land and was occupied by him, although owned by Percy Butterfield.

After many changes of residents it was empty for a time and the Council considered it as Council Offices, but they decided in favour of Church Villa. Between 1945 and 1960 the owner of the house was Mr. Mason, a flamboyant character interested in horse racing who founded the time form method of picking winners.

It continued as a house until 1963 when the owners put in various planning applications for housing developments ranging from 8 detached houses to 26 town houses. In 1964 planning was granted and the house was demolished in 1965 to make way for the town houses on the corner of Sunmead Road and Green Street.

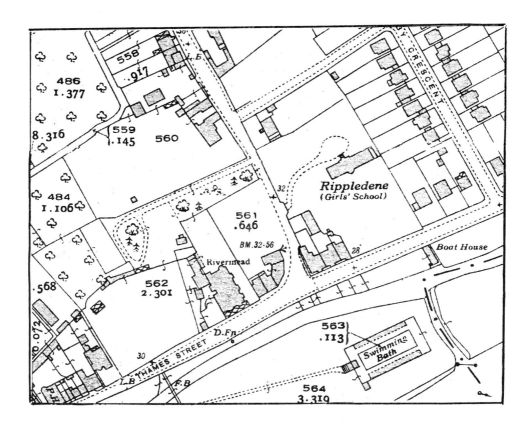

Rosedale was reputed to be a Queen Anne or Georgian house on the site of what is now Elizabeth Gardens (to the right of map ref 560). The first mention of the house is on the 1848 Parish Map when it was owned and occupied by Joseph Turner.

Records show that Henry Richardson lived there from 1878. In the 1891 Census he is listed as a wine merchant living there with his wife Emma, son Henry, also a wine merchant, daughter Eleanor and a visitor, Annie Moore, who was a companion. There were 3 servants in the house (cook, housemaid and parlour maid).

Henry Richardson lived there until at least 1899. Later occupants were Foster Reynolds and Sherard Cowper-Coles who made it his first Sunbury home in 1912. The 1912 Valuation Survey shows that Henry Richardson was still the owner but living in Eastbourne, so presumably he had retired.

The house was demolished to make way for the Elizabeth Gardens development.

Rossall House (formerly Chapel House)   Thames Street

The house is on the 1848 Parish Map and is listed as being owned and occupied by Robert Charsley. From 1859 until 1872 the house had various occupants and was known as Chapel House after the chapel which stood opposite.

After 1874 it was known as Rossall House and became the home of Lady Fleetwood, widow of Sir Peter Fleetwood Bt, of Rossall Hall, Fleetwood, Lancs.

The 1881 Census shows Richard Edwards living there with his son Richard who was a solicitors articled clerk, 2 domestics and 3 servants, although the next Census in 1891 shows John Chandler in residence with his wife and 3 little children. His occupation was domestic gardener, he was probably there as a caretaker.

The 1912 Valuation Survey states the house was owned by R. H. Knight-Bruce of London and occupied by Rev. S. E. Cottam. The stable and coachhouse were opposite the house, presumably on the riverside. In 1937 the Royal Commission on Historical Monuments wrote "Has been much altered but the south front retains modillioned eaves-cornice. Inside the building are some panelling and a staircase with twisted or turned balusters".

A later resident was Sherard Cowper-Coles, founder of Cowper-Coles Aircraft Co. Ltd. which manufactured aircraft components during WWI. He was a brilliant inventor: Electrical, Mechanical and Civil Engineer and a founder member of the Faraday Society. He died in 1936 and is buried in the new cemetery. Mrs. Cowper-Coles continued to live there until it was sold in 1941 to Norman Hewitt a local inventor, who used it as a laboratory. The house was demolished some time after 1955 to make way for flats.

Santa Clara

Santa Clara was a large red brick late Victorian house on the left half way between Thames Street and Manor Lane. Part of the house rose through three floors, and there were tiled decorated bay windows.

One of the early residents was Miss Amy Hutchinson who was there from 1898. By 1903 Dr. Edward Palgrave had moved in but later Miss Hutchinson returned. By 1908, and until the 1912 Valuation Survey, Lt·Col·Thomas Francis Bushe CMG RA lived there. Some time after, it was used as a Christian Scientists nursing home.

Various planning applications were lodged with the Council for alterations from 1937 onwards. In 1958 an application was granted for the demolition of the house and the erection of 4 pairs of semi-detached houses. The photograph was probably taken just before the demolition.

Shamrock Lodge   Vicarage Road

This house stood at the corner of Vicarage Road and Railway Place (now called Windsor Road). The earliest record shows John William Watson living there in 1874. The house had many residents until 1926 when the family of George Frederick Dear moved in and stayed until at least 1933.

Unfortunately no photograph of the house exists, only this one of the garden with two of its occupants in about 1926. They are Alice Dear and her mother, with a friend, Mrs Rolls. In the background can be seen the terraced houses of Railway Place (now all gone).

Southey Cottage   Cadbury Road

Southey Cottage was on the east side of Cadbury Road, just north of Staines Road West, approximately on the site of the flats. The 1848 Parish Map shows that it was owned by Elizabeth Andrews and occupied by Daniel Frisker. There were many occupants of the house until 1900 when William Allen moved in.

The 1912 Valuation Survey shows William Allen as being owner and occupier of the house, stables and paddock covering just over 2 acres. On the ground floor there was a drawing room, dining room, kitchen, scullery, pantry, larder and store room. The 1st floor had 4 bedrooms, bathroom and WC. There is a detailed description of the buildings and outhouses. The house was built of stock bricks with a slated roof and a corrugated iron roofed verandah along the whole of the front. There were lean-to store rooms with tiled roofs, a brick built wash house, a large greenhouse, stables with 3 stalls and 2 loose boxes, harness room, coachhouse, brick pigsties and wooden fowl houses. The house was demolished in about 1960.

Spelthorne Grove

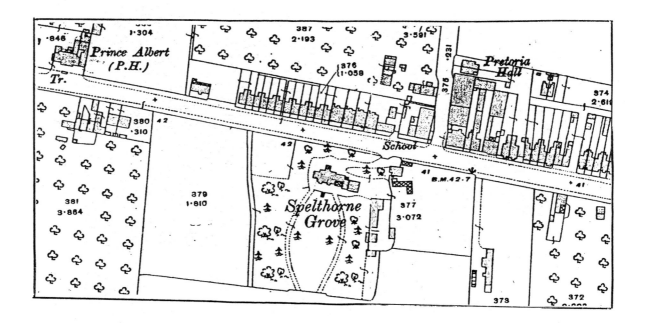

Spelthorne Grove appears to have been built about 1839 for William Alexander Weightman and is shown on the 1848 Parish Map as being owned by Hugh Weightman. Although it changed hands in following years it was unoccupied in 1851 and only had 1 servant as caretaker in residence in 1861. About 1878 it became the home of Robert Cottrill, a landowner, and his family. The 1881 Census tells us that Robert lived there with his wife Charlotte, a son Charles, daughter Mary and his mother-in-law of 70 years. By 1891 his mother-in-law is no longer there and his son is listed as an undergraduate at Oxford Later his son Charles took it over until 1933.

The 1912 Valuation Survey shows that the house, at 114 Staines Road West, was owned by the Cottrills, and set in just over 9 acres of land, including meadow land. The only mention of the actual building was that it had a billiard room.

The 1915 OS map shows it to be a large building, set amid trees with outbuildings and greenhouses. It was demolished to make way for the Spelthorne Grove Estate.

Sunbury House Practical Artillery Institution, Middlesex.

THE PRACTICAL MILITARY INSTITUTE, AT SUNBURY.

Sunbury House   Fordbridge Road

Sunbury House was one of the most important and grand houses in the parish. It was built in the mid 17th century by John Turner on the site of a much older house. The house had a spacious central hall, a double oak staircase carved by Grinling Gibbons, panelling in walnut, and ceilings painted by Verrio in 1706. From 1774 Charles Vere, a banker and art dealer, lived here until 1789 when he sold it to Charles Bishop, whose family owned it for many years.

Charles Bishop was Procurator General to the Army. In his time, George III and the Prince Regent both liked the tranquil setting of the house and were frequent visitors. The 1839 plan shows that the estate had extended to 66 acres and was owned by John Bishop, Charles' son, but by 1848 was owned and occupied by the heirs of John. The 1851 Census shows that the house had 2 gardeners as caretakers of the property.

In 1855 the Bishop family leased Sunbury House to Capt. Auguste Frederick Lendy who, with the assistance of the Orleans family, founded a Military Academy. The Comte de Paris and the Duc de Chartres both graduated from here as did their sons, Louis Phillipe and Henri. Queen Victoria had provided sanctuary in England for the Orleans family in 1848, and often visited Sunbury House when they were there. Another important student was Sir Evelyn Wood who trained there before entering Staff College in 1861.

The Military Academy flourished for many years. The 1861 Census reports that Capt. Lendy, at the age of 35, was the Principal and lived there with his wife Sophia and 2 baby daughters. There were 3 professors and 16 students. 11 of these pupils were listed as Military Students aged 16 to 22 years, but the other 5 aged between 20 and 25 years, were attached to regiments - Capt: 16th Reg., Lieuts: 77th Reg., 96th Regt., 13th Reg., 2nd Dragoon Guards. Gentlemen at the time went into regiments as officers - perhaps these needed some military training before joining their regiments. There were 14 servants attached to the house, (butler, under butler, nursery maid, housemaids, kitchen and laundry maids, cook and gardeners).

By 1871 the Lendy family had grown to 5 children, and there were 11 pupils and 13 servants. In 1881 Auguste Lendy was a Major (retired) and there were 14 students, 4 visitors and 9 servants.

By 1890 Major General Grant Blunt was in charge of the Academy, with Dominic Feeneys assisting as military school tutor, with 10 students, aged 16 to 20 years, and 6 servants.

In 1902 it is recorded that the house had been turned into flats with George Ostreham, previously living in Weir View, as one of the tenants. The 1912 Valuation Survey records that the property covered nearly 9 acres and was owned by John Carnegie of Bucklersbury, London EC. On New Years Eve 1915 the house, which consisted of a central block with 2 wings similar to Sunbury Court, was destroyed by fire. Only the 2 wings were saved and turned into separate houses, one of which was demolished later. The remaining wing, recognised by the pilasters, is now called Sunbury House.

Sunbury Lodge   **Green Street**

Sunbury Lodge Green Street

This substantial Victorian house was built in the first half of the 19th century on about 3 acres of land, with a 12 acre grass meadow, farm buildings and gardens attached. In 1839 and 1848 it was owned by James Slater and occupied by the Rev. Daniel Henry Wall and his wife, Caroline, and 2 servants - all still there in the 1851 Census.

In 1861 Peregrine Birch was the owner occupier. He was a notable Sunbury resident, who was a barrister, a Clerk to the Parliament Office of the House of Lords, and a Director of the Sunbury Gas Company. He lived here with his wife, 6 sons (one of whom was a solicitors articled clerk) and 3 daughters. Also in the household were 2 visiting children, a tutor and 5 servants. Sadly 4 daughters all died young and are buried in the old cemetery. By 1871 1 daughter and 4 sons (one a civil engineer and another in the Stock Exchange) were still at home.

In 1864 Peregrine Birch and Thomas Barnett bought the Kempton Park Estate for £40,000 intending to develop the area, but nothing came of it. In 1874 Peregrine Birch sold Sunbury Lodge to another barrister Frederick Wallroth. The Census of 1881 shows him living there with his wife, 4 little children, a niece, 2 cousins and another barrister, together with 9 servants. By 1891 his 4 children were with him, 2 cousins and 6 servants (cook, butler, housemaids and kitchen maid).

The 1912 Valuation Survey shows the estate to be just over 16 acres including meadow lands, farm buildings and garden land.

The sale of the house in 1920 gives a detailed description - brick built, slate roof, 4 reception rooms, 5 service rooms including housekeepers room and butlers pantry, 6 bedrooms, 2 nurseries, 4 servants bedrooms, bathrooms, WCs, hot and cold water and piped gas. In 1926 it was owned by Miss Holland and later became a hotel. It was bought in 1946, together with surrounding land, by a builder and demolished in 1953 for houses. (When making a new garden in 1956 near the old ditch at the end of the garden of the Lodge many pieces of broken crockery appeared - had the maids disposed of the evidence of their breakages?)

Sunbury Park (formerly Arden House)   Thames Street

A Palladian mansion originally stood on the site, built in 1712. One of the owners, Edmund Boehm, a merchant in London left money to the poor of Sunbury. In about 1848 a double winged, chateau style house was built in its place.

The 1861 Census shows that Richard Edward Arden, Magistrate and Deputy Lieutenant for the County of Middlesex, and a landed proprietor was the owner. He was also a barrister at law, but not practising. He lived there with his wife Mary, son Percy, an undergraduate at Brasenose College, Oxford, daughter Caroline, 2 more sons and 3 more daughters, all scholars. In the household on that day were a sister-in-law (proprietor of railways) and a visitor (oil merchant). There was a governess and 8 servants (butler, footman, nurse, undernurse, cook and housemaids). The Ardens were a prominent local family who continued to live in what was then called Arden House until the 1880's.

Although the house was still owned by the Ardens, the family of Captain George Dennis Sampson were in residence in 1890. The 1891 Census tells us his wife Fanny (living on her own means), 2 young sons, mother-in-law, cousin and a visitor (all living on own means) together with 7 servants (housekeeper, cook, butler, kitchenmaid, nurse, nursemaid and nurse's child), were all residing in the house.

The 1912 Valuation Survey shows the owners as the Ardens and the estate covering just over 33 acres. In the 1914/18 war it was occupied by the Army and in the 1939/45 war by the Fire Service.

In the 1950's it was demolished as being in a ruinous state, although the disused stables were used as garage and piggeries for a while in 1952. The only parts to survive are the walled garden, the wall on Thames Street and the ha-ha.

Tadmor   Halliford Road

This house was built about 1870 for Sidney Billings, reputed to have had dealings with India and the East. Tadmor is the alternative Arabic name for Palmyra and could be connected with his travels. He lived here until his death, after which time his widow continued in residence.

Mrs. Tamzine Billings and her niece Honoria Jones erected the Parish Rooms in memory of her husband Sidney.

The photograph was taken by Mrs.Lethbridge in 1935 during the 3 years she lived in Tadmor. She said this was the view from the front, the door was at the side and the left of the photograph backed on to Halliford Road. The house, which had a reputation for ghosts, was set in about two and a half acres including a field and an orchard.

The land and property were bought by a builder in 1946, the house was demolished and the area was redeveloped into a housing estate which included Tadmor Close.

Weir View

This large early 19th century house was an interesting construction consisting of twin gables running parallel to the river, each being stepped halfway along following the fall of the banking. There was a glazed verandah on the river side with 3 large windows opening on to it. It had an unusual pointed window at the side set below the roof valley, perhaps as a light for the staircase. The first mention of Weir View is on a 1848 Parish Map when it was owned by Elizabeth Warden, but was unoccupied.

In 1865 Edward Lukyn, a dentist, lived there with his wife, Rose, and little daughter Emilie. By the 1871 Census the family had grown - 3 daughters and 2 sons. Edward had died by 1891 and his widow, Rose, continued to live there with 6 of her children, including the elder son, Herbert, who was a medical student.

For the years between 1898 and 1900 there was a break when George William Ostreham, an artist who painted the seraphim and Christ the King on the Chancel walls of St Mary's Church resided in Weir View. After that Herbert Lukyn, now a doctor, took over the house.

The Valuation Survey of Oct.9th 1912 described the house as having a front elevation with a strip of land forming the front garden enclosed by iron railings. There were 3 reception rooms, kitchen, scullery, WC and coal cellar on the ground floor, and 6 bedrooms, a dressing room, bathroom and storeroom on the 1st floor. The garden with a greenhouse was at the side together with a landing stage. At this time the house was in a bad state of repair.

From the 1920's William Langbridge owned the house and later his widow lived there until her death in 1960. Their son applied for planning permission in 1962 to erect a summer house in the garden. Permission was refused and soon after he sold the house to the Council who demolished it to make way for the extension to Kings Lawn Garden. An old wisteria in the riverside garden is all that remains of the old garden.

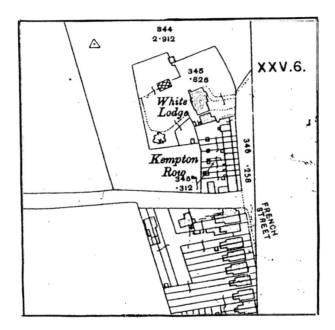

White Lodge was situated at the top of French Street just north of the terrace of cottages (still in existence) called Kempton Row on the site of what is now a factory.

The Misses Jones (Mary, Sara and Lydia) three elderly sisters, whose income was derived from houses and funds, lived in this Victorian house from 1874. Mary, the eldest was, at the age of 87, still living in the house in 1892 looked after by 4 servants (a housemaid, a nurse and two domestics).

The 1912 Valuation Survey showed that it was owned by Mrs.Ella Shaw of Guildford, and the land covered just over 4 acres. Various people are recorded as having lived there until 1937. The house is marked on the 1947 OS map, although there is no record of the demolition date.

Duppa's Farm (Merrick's Farm)   Russell Road

This Victorian farmhouse stood next to Battlecrease Hall in Russell Road. The land was owned by the Duppa Charities, originally founded by Bishop Duppa who had been tutor to Charles II when he was a boy. It was the home for many years of the Merrick family, whose farmyard lay alongside the house. In 1881, Henry Merrick, described as a farmer of 300 acres, employing 23 men, lived at the house with his wife Kate and their son, Henry's brother, and Kate's mother.

By 1891, the farmer was Edward Merrick, who shared the house with his wife Clara, 5 sons and 2 daughters. The older children had all been born at Ashford (Middx.), so presumably the family had farmed there before taking over the farm from Henry Merrick.

The last Merricks to farm there were Horace and Winifred, who gave up the farm in 1955. The Duppa's Trust decided to sell the farmland for development - Thamesmead School playing fields are the only survivor of the open space, the rest having been developed for housing.

Joy Hoole, who lived at the house after the Merricks, reports that after the farm closed, the rats moved into the house. The Hooles left soon afterwards! Development of the house and farmyard itself was delayed by its being on the route of the projected Shepperton Eastern bypass. Another factor was a residential caravan site which had been on part of the land since the 1930's. Various schemes were proposed, including a residential care home for children, but the site was eventually developed for housing in the 1980's as Duppa's Village.

Fairleigh was a Victorian house situated on the west side of the High Street (formerly Highfield Road). It was built about the same time as Highfield and the Lindsay estate cottages.

The 1871 Census gives the occupier as Albert Mallalieu, 28, a Landowner, together with his wife Annie, a daughter, his mother-in-law and 2 servants.

In 1881, William Whinfield, a coal merchant, aged 56, had taken over the house, with his wife Eliza, 2 sons, 3 daughters and 2 servants. He was still living at the house in 1891, but one son had left home. The remaining son was employed as a clerk at Lincrusta, London. This was a company formed by Frederick Walton of Staines Linoleum fame, to produce decorative wall coverings. The factory was in Hanworth Road, Sunbury. When the company was registered in 1880, two of the original shareholders were William and John Whinfield of Fairleigh.

In 1915, the property was recorded as being owned by Sir Richard Burbidge of Littleton Park (and chairman of Harrods). The property was presumably rented out. It consisted of a hall, 2 reception rooms, kitchen, larder and pantry on the ground floor, with cellars under. Upstairs were 3 bedrooms, a bathroom and WC, with a further floor containing another 3 bedrooms. The property was demolished in the 1970's, to be replaced by Bishop's Supermarket, now Budgens.

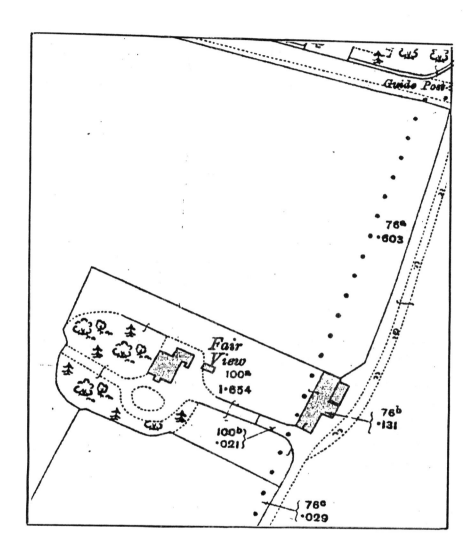

This house lay to the south of Laleham Road, but unusually faced away from the main road, being approached by a driveway, now called Fairview Drive. In 1908 the house was owned by a farmer called Bravington. A George Bravington had been recorded in the 1891 Census at Littleton Farm, and this may well be the same family. Fairview itself seems to have been built around the turn of the century, and does not appear in the 1891 Census.

Elizabeth Smeeth lived at the house with her mother for a short time in 1949, and recalls that it had been divided into flats by Sunbury Urban District Council. She remembers that a hall and stairway divided the ground floor, which was used by two families, whilst the Smeeths and another family lived upstairs. Outside, there was a turning circle for carriages before the front door, and extensive grounds including ornamental trees and an orchard. The house must have been demolished soon afterwards to make way for council housing - the name of the Bravington family lives on in Bravington Close which now occupies the site.

Fernleigh (formerly Heathfield)   Manygate Lane

One of the estate of 'Villas' built on the west side of Manygate Lane (identified as 'Villa Road' in the 1881 census) by the Lindsay Estate.

The occupier in 1881 was Theodore Bullock, an ironfounder, together with his wife and 2 servants. In 1891, it was Edward Moore, a chartered accountant. A widower, he lived at the house with 3 servants. By the time of the 1915 Valuation Survey, the house had become 'Fernleigh', and was occupied by P. Honnor, agent to the Lindsay Estate, which still owned the property. It was described as having 3 reception rooms, a kitchen, scullery and conservatory on the ground floor, with 4 bedrooms, a bathroom and boxroom above. In 1948, it became the home of Terrick & Mary Fitzhugh. Terrick was a co-founder of the Sunbury & Shepperton Local History Society in 1951. They leased the building from the Lindsay Estate, but were persuaded to relinquish the remainder of the lease in 1963 to the Lyon Group, property developers, who had already acquired the other Lindsay Estate houses nearby. A couple of days after moving out, they returned to find their former home a pile of rubble! An estsate of townhouses was built on the site, at prices ranging from £5,250 for a studio house to £9,250 for a 3-storey terraced townhouse.

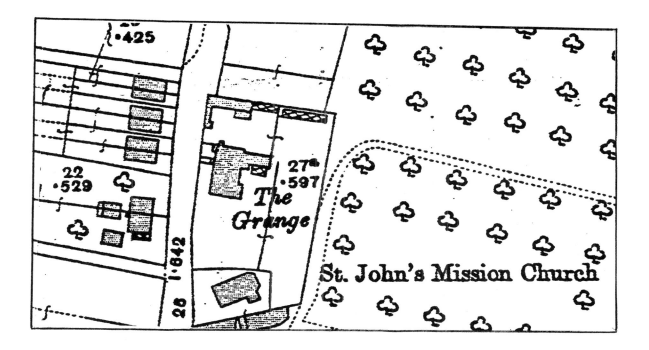

The Grange stood on the east side of Watersplash Road, just north of the former St. Johns Mission Church (built 1870) which was sited immediately opposite Petts Lane. Its date of construction is uncertain, but it appears in the 1861 Census as in the possession of John Lea, described as a Batchelor of Arts (Oxford) and fund holder. He lived at the house with his wife Latitia, a son and daughter and 4 servants.

The 1871 Census lists Herman Zobel, 50, born in Wurtemburg, Germany, and a Professor of Mathematics, as the occupier. He shared the house with his wife Sofia, 3 daughters, 3 sons and 3 male pupils, together with one servant. He was still at The Grange in 1891, but now described as a military tutor. It is tempting to speculate that he may have taught at Captain Lendy's Military Academy at Sunbury House.

In the 1915 Valuation Survey, Samuel Garved is listed as the occupier, the Rev. Gidney having deceased. It is not clear why the Rev. Gidney, Rector of Shepperton 1904-1913 should have lived here rather than Shepperton Rectory. The house was owned by Trustees led by the Rev. Frederick Salt (Rector of Shepperton 1913-1927), and had been left to the Church (presumably by the Rev. Gidney?).

The Grange seems to have been demolished in the late 1950's or early 1960's, and was replaced by a development of senior citizens' bungalows, appropriately named 'Grange Court'.

The Grove

The Grove was one of the estate of detached houses built by the Lindsay Estate. It was situated on the north side of Grove Road, off Manygate Lane, and was replaced by townhouses in the 1960's.

The 1891 Census recorded the occupant as Bryan Whitmore, 53, described as a landscape painter, together with his wife Henrietta and one servant. In 1915, Henrietta, by now a widow, was still living there. She held the house on a 99 year lease from the Lindsay Estate, starting from September 1883 (presumably when the house was built).

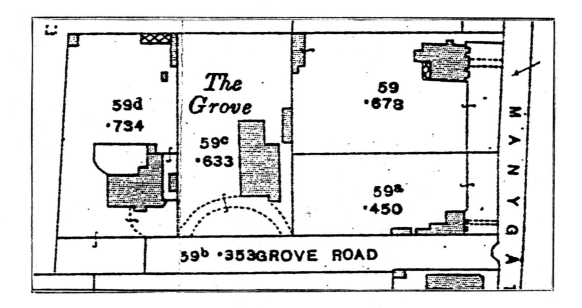

Copthorne

Copthorne stood next to The Grove on the north side of Grove Copthorne Road.

It does not appear by name in the 1891 census, but the 1915 Valuation Survey records the occupier as an E.W. Clisby, and the owner as Charles Kensington of Goring, Oxfordshire. It was valued at £1465.

The house was demolished at the same time as The Grove, and the site is now occupied by the bungalows of Copthorne Close, off Grove Road.

Halliford Bend   Russell Road
(later Hotel Andra, Thames Riviera Hotel, Riverview Hotel)

This property, which stood on the corner of Manygate Lane, had a very varied history. Originally built as a private house, probably in the late 18th century, it was considerably modified and added to in the Victorian era. The photograph taken across the river must date from before 1910, as there is no Dial House to the left of the house, then called Halliford Bend. Note the unusual horizontal louvres or blinds at the windows. In the small riverside garden are a thatched summerhouse and boathouse. Also visible, just at the edge of the river, are the inverted 'V' shape supports used to support the 'greasy pole' at Shepperton Regatta (you had to get from one end of the pole to the other without falling in - few did!).

In the second photograph, we see the building in 1943, having become the 'Hotel Andra' in the 1930's. The roof had been rebuilt to a 'mansard' form, with the upper storey windows now dormers. It had also acquired a somewhat dubious reputation!

By 1961, the hotel had changed its name to the Thames Riviera Hotel Club, and in 1966 application was made to build a new 40 bedroom hotel on the site. This was refused, and another name change had taken place by 1968, to the Riverview Hotel. After a disastrous fire in the early 1980's, plans were approved to demolish the hotel and replace it with a large block of 3 and 4-storey flats.

Halliford Hoo (Halliford Cottage)   Russell Road

This unusual Regency villa, dating from the early 19th century, was situated on the north side of Russell Road, alongside The Lodge . The photograph taken in July 1943 shows the building set in extensive grounds, with a frontage of 200 feet to Russell Road, and extending back for 500 feet. Some of the large trees were preserved in the new housing estate.

Like The Lodge , Halliford Hoo (also known as Halliford Cottage) was also owned by the Russell family. In 1891, the occupier was William Scott, a stockbroker. In 1915, Mrs Ada Russell was the owner, and the property was recorded as having an entrance hall, large drawing room, dining room, morning room, kitchen, scullery, dairy, housekeeper's room, servants bedroom, pantry, larder, wine and coal cellars, as well as 5 bedrooms. Stabling consisted of 2 stalls, a coach house and 2 timber built cow houses.

Although seemingly a single-storey building, the house was in fact built on a knoll and was of 2 stories to the rear.

Like The Lodge , it was demolished in the early 1960's to make way for the new Mulberry Trees housing estate. The name of this estate commemorates the trees which stood in the grounds of the old house.

Halliford House

Halliford House was situated on the east side of Upper Halliford Road, and the remnants of its original 36 acres of grounds are now a public park.

The house was built in the 18th century, with later additions. A directory of 1839 lists a Mrs. Everard as living at the house, but in 1841 Dr. Joseph Seaton founded a private mental hospital there. It catered for the 'upper classes', and advertised that it took voluntary, temporary and certified patients.

Dr. Seaton was there for many years; in 1871, the Census listed him as being a widower, living at the house with 3 daughters and a son, 11 staff and 21 patients (12 female, 9 male). In the Census, the latter are only identified by initials, which gives some idea of the stigma attached to mental illness at the time.

By the 1891 Census, Dr. David Edwards was in charge of 12 servants, 15 female patients and 12 male patients. There had obviously been a change of attitude, as all the patients were now listed under their full names. The matron, Jane Rogers, was recorded as having been born at the Tower of London.

An 1894 directory gives the superintendent's name as Dr. William Haslett. A member of Sunbury Urban District Council, he was also the doctor at the Sunbury Nursing Home in Sunbury village, an establishment founded by a Mrs. Blaney around the turn of the century. Obviously a pillar of the local community, he is said to have married one of his wealthier patients!

A brochure for the hospital, dating from the 1920's or 30's, states that patients had separate bedrooms, and milk and vegetables were supplied by the establishments' own farm. The system of treatment was described as being 'entirely domestic in nature, the utmost liberty consistent with the safety of the patient is permitted'. Although referred to in a 1937 directory, it is not clear how long the asylum lasted. The house was demolished in the early 1950's, and the only remnants are the gate piers, re-located to a house on the corner of Halliford Road in Upper Halliford. Within the park, a mound marks the site of the house, and trees remain from the circular drive which led from Upper Halliford Road.

The early 19th century print (opposite) shows the house from the lawn to the north. A low fence divides the garden from the pasture beyond.

The chauffeur next to the car is nineteen year-old Donald Clifton, pictured in 1914 outside the garage converted from the former stables, which appear to the south on the plan. The car appears to be a 15HP Napier.

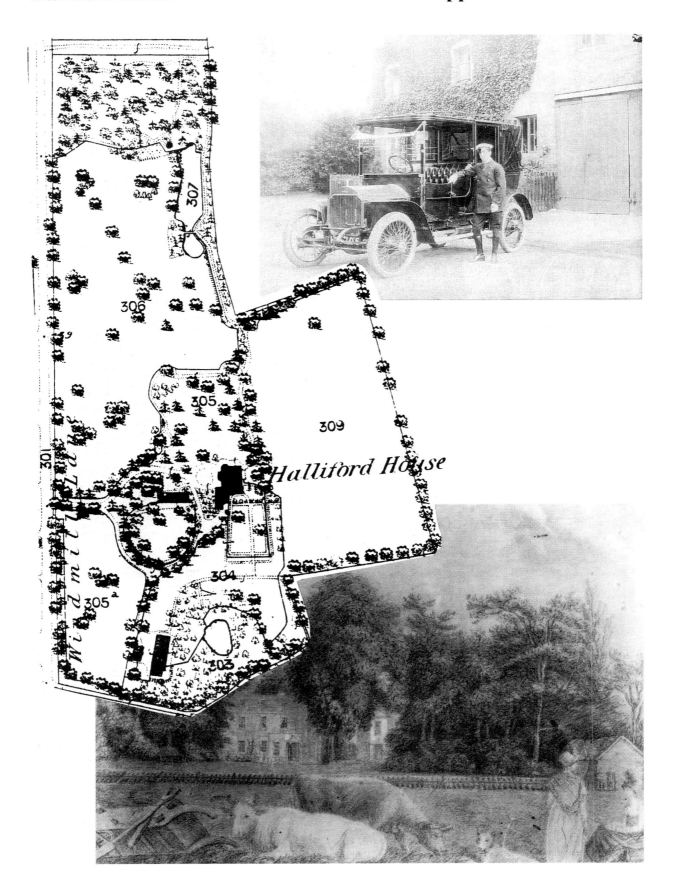

This building stood on the west side of the High Street (formerly Highfield Road). It was built in the latter part of the 19th century by the Lindsay estate, at the same time as the pair of estate cottages. All have now disappeared, replaced by blocks of flats and maisonettes in the 1950's. It stood quite close to the road on a narrow plot which opened out to an 'L' shape behind Fairleigh, the neighbouring property.

In 1881, the occupants were Edwin Roper, 25, a General Practitioner, together with his wife Harriet, 26, and two servants. By 1891, a son and 3 daughters had been added to the household. The house was leased from the Lindsay estate; by 1915, the occupier was a Mr. Townsend.

The house consisted of 3 reception rooms, a kitchen, scullery, larder and WC on the ground floor, with 4 bedrooms, a bathroom and WC upstairs. At the rear of the property was a stable with two stalls, and two coach houses.

Italian Villa stood on Chertsey Road opposite Ferry Lane. The site is now occupied by flats called 'Norman House'. The photograph shows the house, built about 1850, to have had an external veranda and typically elaborate Victorian gardens.

In the 1881 Census, the occupants were listed as James and Jane Boor with their nieces Mary and Elizabeth O'Donnell, the last three of Irish birth. James Boor was living on his investments. He died in 1887, and there is a plaque in his memory in Shepperton Church, placed there by the three Masonic Lodges (St. Georges and Abbey, Chertsey, and Thames Valley, Halliford) of which he was a prominent member. He was also a Churchwarden at Shepperton, and the lectern, a brass eagle, was presented by his widow in 1889. Both of them are commemorated by the chancel screen, erected in 1911 by their nieces. In the 1891 Census, his widow was still living at the house with her nieces. The O'Donnell sisters were remembered in their turn by a stained glass window erected in the church in 1952.

By the time of the 1915 Valuation Survey, the two O'Donnell sisters had inherited the property (held freehold) and were both still living there. The house consisted of 2 sitting rooms, a kitchen and scullery plus 'usual offices' on the ground floor, with 4 bedrooms, a bathroom and WC on the first floor. Outside, stabling for 2 horses and a coach house (unusable!) were recorded. The property was valued at £850.

Kilmiston House   Manygate Lane

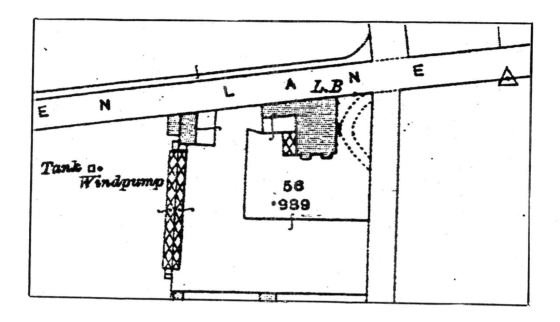

Kilmiston House stood on the corner of Manygate Lane and Green Lane, and was one of the substantial detached houses built in the 1880's by the Lindsay estate. (William Schaw Lindsay had been Lord of the Manor of Shepperton from 1856 until his death in 1877, being succeeded by his grandson, Colonel M.E.Lindsay.) The 1891 Census lists the occupants as John Roberts, 44, a nurseryman, his wife Florence and two sons. They presumably moved on fairly soon, as a gravestone in Shepperton cemetery records that a Margaret McDonald died at the house on the 6th August 1901.

By the time of the 1915 Valuation Survey, a Mr. Robbins was living in the house, the owner of the property still being the Lindsay estate. The property was described as having 3 reception rooms, a kitchen, scullery, larder, pantry, washhouse and lavatory downstairs, whilst upstairs there were 5 bedrooms, a dressing room, bathroom and WC. At the back of the house was stabling for two horses, and a coach house with lofts above.

During the Second World War, the house was used as offices by Thomas Headley & Co., and after the war various schemes were put forward for housing on the site. At first, it was proposed to build on the site of the stables and retain the house, but after numerous applications, a scheme to replace the house with a 2-storey block of 10 flats was approved in 1964. The development was completed by 1966, and the new flats took on the name of Kilmiston House.

Littleton Rectory   Squire's Bridge Road

Littleton Rectory was built in 1699, and although this was during the last few years of the reign of William III, it was typical of the style known as 'Queen Anne', after his successor. The photograph shows the steep hipped roof and symmetrical design typical of this era, though with later additions such as the front bay windows and the cluster of outbuildings at the rear. The elaborate topiary in front of the house is noteworthy. The cedar tree survives in the grounds of the present rectory, which was built in 1968, together with two rows of terraced houses behind it called Rectory Close. This was part of the plan to build the new Littleton Infants' School, to replace the Old School on the other side of the main road. Incredibly, it was also considered purchasing, and possibly demolishing, the adjacent Old Manor House and grounds to add to the new school site.

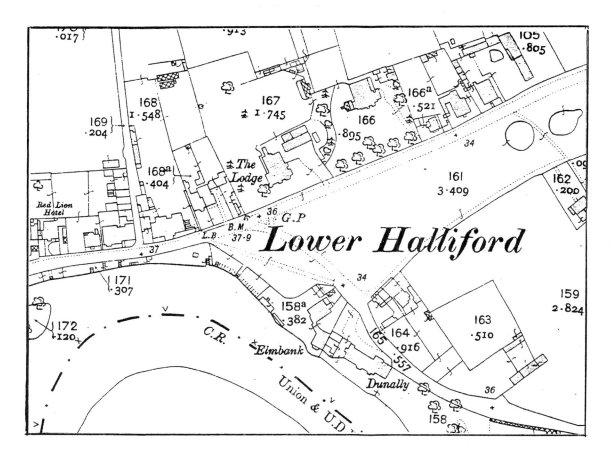

This house, dating from the 19th century, stood on the north side of Russell Road, facing Lower Halliford Green, on the site now occupied by the 'Mulberry Trees' estate.

The 1861 Census lists John Cunningham, 50, gentleman, as being resident with his wife Mary, 2 daughters and 1 servant. In 1871 John and Ada Russell were living at The Lodge , together with their 3 daughters, 1 son and 5 servants.

By 1881 another son had been added to the household, and John Russell was described as a civil servant.

It seems that Mrs Russell had been widowed by 1915, as the Valuation Survey in that year gives her as the owner of the property. The house is described as having a large hall, dining and drawing rooms, study, housekeeper's room, kitchen, scullery, pantry and boot room on the ground floor, with coal and wine cellars below. Upstairs were 5 small and 2 large bedrooms, 2 bathrooms and a WC.

Outside there were stabling for 5 horses, a loose box, harness room and a double coach house with rooms over. There was also a hothouse for growing tender plants. The whole property was valued at £2400.

By 1955, permission had been given to convert The Lodge and the adjoining coach house to 6 flats with garages, but in 1961, a scheme to build houses on the site was passed by the Council. A further scheme was refused in 1964, as part of the land was required for the route of the Shepperton bypass (to run from Marshall's Roundabout north of Walton Bridge, and behind properties in Russell Road, to link near the war memorial with the western bypass). Although the western part was eventually built as Renfree Way, the eastern part was abandoned, and thus permission was finally given to build the Mulberry Trees estate.

Manor Farm   Chertsey Road

Manor Farm was located on the north side of Chertsey Road, and was the principal farm belonging to the estate of the Lord of the Manor. As such, the property had a history stretching back to the Domesday Survey of 1086, but the last farmhouse on the site seems to have dated from the 18th century.

The 1841 Census records the occupiers as John Sanders, 35, a yeoman farmer, his wife Ann, 7 daughters, 2 sons and 5 servants - obviously a substantial house is indicated!

In 1861, the Census gives the farmer as Richard Fladgate, 44, who lived at the farm with his wife Susannah and two servants.

By 1871, the occupier was William Merrick, who was still there in 1891 at the age of 51, living with his wife Louisa and 2 sons. It is interesting to note how the number of servants had now declined to none. In 1915, Mr. D. Crawford and Mr. Melville were at the farm, which was still owned by the Lindsay estate. By then, the farm consisted of 325 acres of land, and included 4 cottages. It was valued at £33,167, a considerable sum for the time and by far the most valuable property in Shepperton.

The photograph dates from August 1943 and shows an attractive Georgian house with a prominent triangular pediment - quite elaborate for a farmhouse and no doubt reflecting its position as the Manor Farm.

By 1946, application had been made to Sunbury Urban District Council to erect a smaller, more modern farmhouse, as it was claimed that the existing building was too large and uneconomical to run. The applicant had to make a case for building a new house exceeding the maximum size allowed, presumably due to post-war restraints on the use of building materials. By 1958 however, plans were submitted to build 58 houses on the site. This was refused, but a later application was granted. A fine 17th century barn that stood on the site was also demolished. The extension to the St. Nicholas Drive estate was eventually built on the land.

Pembury House (formerly Westfield)   Manygate Lane

One of the large detached houses erected by the Lindsay Estate in the latter part of the 19th century, Pembury House was sited near the junction with the present Grove Road. The photograph shows that there was extensive accommodation on 2 floors, with attic rooms above. Note the unmade surface of Manygate Lane, and the recently planted trees which are now mature and such a feature of the road.

In 1881, the property then known as Westfield House was a small school, with a staff of 3 governesses (one French, one German) and 4 resident scholars aged between 11 and 16. By 1891, it was the home of Robert Holborn, 'living on his own means', together with his wife Sarah, 2 sons and 2 servants. In 1915, the name had changed to Pembury House and the Valuation Survey noted the occupier as A. Vernon, whilst the owner was T. W. Vincent, of The Dairy, Shepperton.

Like the other nearby houses, Pembury House was demolished in about 1963 to make way for the townhouses which now occupy the west side of Manygate Lane.

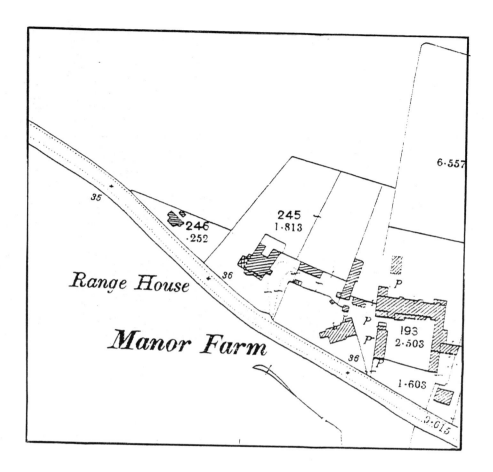

This house stood on the north side of Chertsey Road, next to Manor Farm (q.v.) and right at the edge of the village of Shepperton. It was built about 1875, by the Lindsay estate, who seem to have been involved in extensive house building at the time.

In the 1891 Census, the occupants were Edward Steele, 72, a retired civil servant, his wife Christian, one daughter and three servants. A coachman occupied a cottage on the property.

By the time of the 1915 Valuation Survey, the property was vacant, although still owned by the Lindsay estate. The accommodation was listed as a detached brick and slate house, consisting of 2 large and 1 small reception rooms, a conservatory, kitchen and scullery on the ground floor. On the first floor were 2 large and 4 small bedrooms, 2 dressing rooms, a bathroom and WC. Above this were 5 attic rooms and a tank room. There were also cellars under the house. Stabling had provision for 3 horses, together with a coach house and tack room, with rooms over.

Planning permission was given in 1960 to replace the house with 10 detached and 4 semi-detached houses together with a new road, and the site is now Range Way.

Shepperton House   Church Road

Shepperton House stood on the bend in Church Road, facing Winches Cottage . The site is now occupied by La Macarena , Woodcote and Senwick .

The house seen in the photograph appears to be of 18th century date, and is quite elaborate with a Venetian window above the porch, and an unusual pediment with an oval plaque on it. Note also the urns on the end of the gables.

It was the home for many years of the Winch family, who besides being farmers, had a business hiring out horses to tow barges on the river. The 1839 list of property owners in Shepperton shows that the largest landowner after the then Lord of the Manor, James Scott, was Juliet Winch, who lived at Shepperton House. She was the daughter of George Winch who had settled in Shepperton in the 18th Century.

In the 1861 Census, Juliet Winch, now 68 (and still unmarried) was still living at the house with a niece and one servant. Ten years later, the occupant was John Winch, 77, with his wife Mary and four daughters. By 1881, John had died but his widow Mary was still living there with her daughters. In 1891, Elizabeth Winch, a widow of 59, was in residence, with two daughters who had both been born in Sydney, Australia. Presumably the family had returned from there to Shepperton.

The 1915 Valuation Survey gives the occupier as a G. Exton. The property was described as a 'very old brick and tile house, formerly a farmhouse'. The accommodation comprised 3 reception rooms, a kitchen, scullery and the 'usual offices' on the ground floor, with 4 bedrooms, dressing room, bathroom and WC upstairs. There were also 2 attic rooms. Stabling consisted of a brick and pantiled stable with two stalls and a coach house. The house was unfortunately gutted in a fire just before the Second World War. It was not rebuilt, and when planning permission was given for a bungalow in 1953, the site was stated to be vacant.

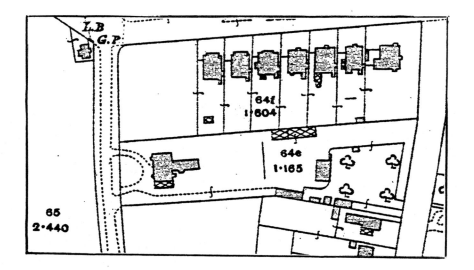

Unusually, in addition to a change of name, Thurlestone underwent a change of road! The 1922 Valuation Survey shows that the house was originally called Lyminge , and listed as part of Broadlands Avenue. The occupier was Mrs. H. Hyamiason, who also held the freehold. As can be seen from the map of 1915, the property stretched between Broadlands Avenue and Highfield Road (now High Street).

It consisted of a drawing room, dining room, morning room, kitchen, scullery and pantry downstairs, whilst above were nine bedrooms and attendant bathrooms. A conservatory stood on the south side of the house, and in the garden were greenhouses and a forcing house (to bring on early crops of fruit or vegetables). The garden was recorded as containing 50 fruit trees. The surveyor in 1922 described the property as 'an exceedingly nice house, substantially built, in perfect order'. He valued it at £1460.

Permission was granted in 1957 for conversion of the house to six flats for a period of five years. A supporting letter from Shepperton Builders stated that the building had been acquired in 1954 for business premises, but that it had been lying derelict almost ever since, except for use by the school. This is presumably a reference to St. Nicholas School, which was chronically short of space until new buildings were opened in Manor Farm Avenue in the mid 1950's.

Reference is also made to the construction of shops in the High Street - Shepperton Builders were at that time constructing six shops opposite to Thurlestone, and it was considered that with another 5 or 6 shops between Green Lane and Thurlestone, this would be all the shops that the population would stand for the next five or six years! In the event, Thurlestone was eventually replaced in the 1960's by the terrace of shops and maisonettes called Thurlestone Parade, together with the houses in Thurlestone Close. A cedar tree which once stood in the garden is still a prominent feature of the High Street, in front of the launderette.

The famous architectural historian, Sir Niklaus Pevsner, described White Cottage as 'a particularly attractive brick and timber-framed cottage'. It stood to the north of The Grange in Watersplash Road. It appears to have been of 17th century date and is said to have been converted from a cow shed.

The 1861 census records the occupier as Samuel Brown, a cowkeeper, and Mary Brown, a laundress. Their daughter Frances, aged 20, was also a laundress. Frances was the occupier in 1881 and 1891, her parents presumably having died. She lived at the house with 3 nieces in 1881. By 1891, there were only two nieces, but it is interesting to note that one of them, Constance (aged 15!) was a teacher in the National School (later St. Nicholas School, but then situated in what is now the 'School of Spice' Indian restaurant). The other niece, Dora, helped with the laundry. Miss Brown was still at the cottage in 1915, when she was paying rent of £11. 14s. 0d. to George Leonard of Staines Road Farm.

The last occupants were Walter and Helen Hone. Walter had a boat business in Weybridge, whilst Helen worked at the Ship Hotel in Russell Road. Walter was later a gateman at Sound City (Shepperton Studios).

The house was acquired by Shepperton Builders in the late 1950's. It was claimed that the building was dilapidated, and the Council Sanitary Inspector was asked to condemn it. Planning Permission for a block of four maisonettes was eventually granted in 1959. Walter and Helen were moved up the road whilst the cottage was demolished and replaced by the block of maisonettes, one of which became their new home.

**Other publications from the
Sunbury and Shepperton Local History Society**

Shepperton Story: Valerie Brooking

A History of Sunbury-on-Thames: George Freeman

Sunbury, Shepperton and the Thames Valley Railway: Kenneth Y. Heselton

A History of Sunbury's Pubs: Kenneth Y. Heselton

Sunbury Inclosure 1800: Nan Trimble

Walks Around Shepperton: Valerie Brooking

Property Owners of Shepperton in 1839

Sunbury: Echoes from the Past Vol. 1: Kenneth Y. Heselton

Sunbury: Echoes from the Past Vol. 2: Kenneth Y. Heselton

Property Owners and Tenants of Sunbury in 1848

The Royal Manor of Kempton from 1086 to 1993: Kenneth Y. Heselton

Shepperton: W. S. Lindsay (first published in 1867)

Shepperton Island Dwellers: compiled by Valerie Brooking

A Shepperton Diary 1907: Edward Rosewell (ed. Valerie Brooking)

Life on the Thames Yesterday & Today (ed. Nan Trimble)

Sunbury Remembered (ed. Nan Trimble)